Diary of a Dog Walker

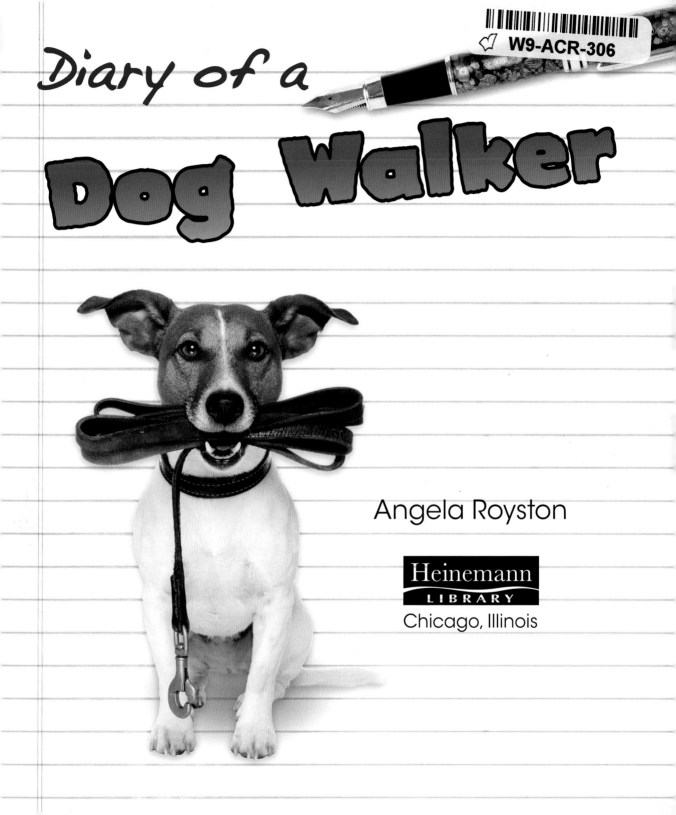

Angela Royston

Heinemann
LIBRARY
Chicago, Illinois

Edited by Daniel Nunn, Rebecca Rissman, and Catherine Veitch
Designed by Cynthia Akiyoshi
Picture research by Ruth Blair
Production by Victoria Fitzgerald
Originated by Capstone Global Library Ltd
Printed and bound in China by South China Printing Company Ltd

17 16 15 14 13
10 9 8 7 6 5 4 3 2 1

Library of Congress Cataloging-in-Publication Data
Royston, Angela, 1945-
  Dog walker / Angela Royston.
    pages cm—(Diary of a . . .)
  Includes bibliographical references and index.
  ISBN 978-1-4329-7581-4 (hb)—ISBN 978-1-4329-7588-3 (pb)
1. Dog walking—Anecdotes. 2. Dogs—Services for—Anecdotes.
I. Title.

SF427.46.R69 2014
636.7'083—dc23   2012046858

Acknowledgments
We would like to thank the following for permission to reproduce
photographs: Corbis pp. 6 (© DK Limited), 8 (© Juice Images),
13 (© VStock LLC/Tetra Images), 22 (© Cristina Estadella), 23
(© Ocean), 24 (© Lawrence Manning); Getty Images pp. 4
(Flickr), 18 (Ingrid Firmhofer), 20 (Nick Ridley/Oxford Scientific);
Shutterstock pp. title page (© Javier Brosch), contents page (©
Lobke Peers), 5 (© Christian Mueller), 7 (© leungchopan), 10
(© Alexander Chaikin), 12 (© cynoclub), 14 (© piotrwzk), 15
(© tim elliott), 16 (© zhu difeng), 19 (© Dmitriy Shironosov), 21
(© Monkey Business Images), 25 (© Lobke Peers), 26 (© Elena
Elisseeva), 27 (© Gina Callaway), 28 pen (© Piligrim), 28 diary
(© Shchipkova Elena); Superstock pp. 9 (Pietro Scozzari / age
fotostock), 11 (F1 ONLINE), 17 (Juniors).

Background and design features reproduced with permission
of Shutterstock. Cover photograph of woman walking dogs
reproduced with permission of Getty Images (Brand X Pictures).

We would like to thank Emily Brummer for her invaluable help in
the preparation of this book.

Every effort has been made to contact copyright holders of
material reproduced in this book. Any omissions will be rectified
in subsequent printings if notice is given to the publisher.

All the Internet addresses (URLs) given in this book were valid at
the time of going to press. However, due to the dynamic nature
of the Internet, some addresses may have changed, or sites may
have changed or ceased to exist since publication. While the
author and publisher regret any inconvenience this may cause
readers, no responsibility for any such changes can be accepted
by either the author or the publisher.

Some words are shown in bold, **like this**. You can find
out what they mean by looking in the Glossary.

Contents

Lots of Dogs

I **earn a living** by walking other people's dogs. Most of the dogs' owners work during the day, so they can't take their dogs for a walk themselves. I walk several groups of dogs.

This is one of my regular groups of dogs.

The dogs never get tired of chasing the ball and bringing it back to me!

I take the dogs to one of the local parks.
The dogs run around and sniff all the smells.
I enjoy my work and have decided to
keep a diary to tell you about it.

Dashing Dogs

Tuesday, June 12

As usual, I picked up each dog from its home. As soon as they saw me, the dogs knew they were going for a walk. They jumped into my car and off we went.

Cages in the back of my car stop the dogs from jumping into the front.

When I let the dogs out, they were very excited. Cindy the dachshund ran off—but she came back at once when I blew the **dog whistle**. I rewarded her with a treat.

Meeting Friends

Wednesday, June 13

My friend Tina is a dog walker, too. We often walk our dogs together. I know all her dogs, and she knows mine. We help each other when there is a problem.

The dogs like to meet each other.

She told me that she has to go to the dentist next Thursday. She asked me if I could walk her dogs that morning. I agreed because she always helps me when I need it.

Sleepover

Sometimes one of the dogs stays with me for a few nights. The owners know that their dog will be cared for and happy while they are away.

Duke is staying at my house tonight. Duke's owner brought his bed and his favorite blanket and toy along with him. Duke soon felt at home and went to sleep.

A Difficult Day

Thursday, June 14

Today was a bad day! This morning a woman in the park said I had too many dogs. I explained that I am a **registered** dog walker and I am allowed to walk six dogs.

The woman's dog was barking a lot.

I once took an animal first-aid class. I learned how to treat injured animals.

She wouldn't listen, and her dog kept growling at Duke. Then I noticed that her dog had a sore paw, so I cleaned it and bandaged it. The woman didn't even thank me!

Rain, Rain, Rain

Friday, June 15

It rained heavily all afternoon today. The dogs didn't mind—they love the puddles and the mud. I had some very wet dogs to dry when we got back from our walk!

I always take each dog back to its home. I have keys to each house, in case the owners are out. As usual, I made sure each dog was settled and had plenty of water to drink before I left.

The Weekend at Last

Saturday, June 16

Many of the owners walk their own dogs on the weekends, so I don't have as many dogs. I replied to my e-mails and checked that everyone had paid me.

In the afternoon, I visited a local **dog show**.
I met lots of my friends and we talked
about dogs! I bought some things for the
dogs from a **booth** there.

Wonderful Walks

Sunday, June 17

I never go to the parks on a Sunday—they are too busy! There are always lots of people in the park, but on Sundays there are three times as many.

I drove to my friend Maria's home in the country instead. There is a quiet place to walk near her house, with a nice path and fields. The dogs love it.

At the Vet's Office

Monday, June 18

I took Sasha the spaniel to her appointment at the **vet** this morning. She had her **annual booster shot** to stop her from getting some dog illnesses.

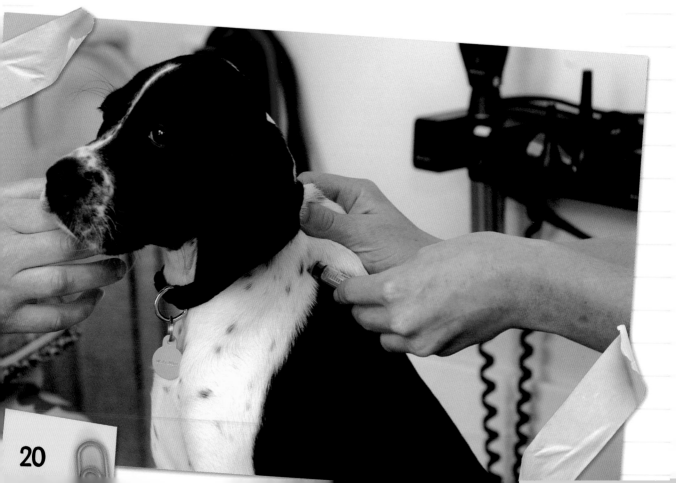

The vet said I was good with animals and should train to be a **veterinary nurse**. She said I could work for them while I train. I'm tempted, but I need to think about it.

What Next?

Should I become a **veterinary nurse**? I like being my own boss, so perhaps Tina and I should start a **business** together. We could employ other dog walkers.

Maybe we could build **kennels** and take care of more dogs when their owners are away. It would cost a lot of money to build the kennels, but we would get paid well by the owners for taking care of their pets.

Playing in the Park

Tuesday, June 19

I took the car into the garage for some repairs this morning. I walked some of the dogs to the park. Tina picked up the other dogs for me in her van.

I met Tina at the park. We let some of the
dogs off their **leashes**. Sammy loves the park.
He picked up a stick and ran around the
park with it.

The Real Reward

It took a while to walk each dog back to its home. One of the dog owners paid me today. He said how grateful he and his wife are that I walk their dog.

Being paid is a good feeling, but seeing the dogs tired and happy after a walk is even better. That's the real reward!

Writing a Diary

I keep a chart of the dogs and the days and times that I walk them. Writing a diary is different. Your diary can describe your life—what you saw, what you felt, and the events that happened.

You can write a secret diary that no one else is supposed to read, or you can write a story in the form of a diary. You could even write an imaginary diary for one of your pets!

Here are some tips for writing a diary:

 Start each entry with the day and the date. You don't have to include an entry for every day.

 The entries should be in **chronological** order, which means that they follow the order in which events happened.

 Use the past tense when you are writing about something that has already happened.

 Remember that a diary is the writer's story, so use "I" and "my."

Glossary

annual every year

booster shot shot to prevent disease, it is given to build upon a previous shot

booth temporary store counter, where things are sold

business organization that sells goods or services to customers

chronological in order of time

dog show competition between different types of dog. The winner is the dog that the judges think is the best looking of that type of dog.

dog whistle whistle that dogs can hear but humans cannot hear

earn a living make enough money to live on

kennel place for keeping dogs, where each dog has its own cage

leash strap that is put around a dog's neck to keep the dog under control

registered approved of by a local government or official organization

vet short for "veterinarian," a doctor for animals

veterinary nurse assistant who is trained to care for sick or injured animals

Find Out More

Books

Buchwald, Claire. *Are You Ready for Me?* (Sit! Stay!). Edina, Minn.: Gryphon, 2007.

Simon, Seymour. *Dogs* (Smithsonian). New York: Collins, 2009.

Whitehead, Sarah. *How to Speak Dog!* New York: Scholastic, 2008.

Internet sites

Facthound offers a safe, fun way to find Internet sites related to this book. All of the sites on Facthound have been researched by our staff.

Here's all you do:
Visit www.facthound.com
Type in this code: 9781432975814

Index